A Guide for Using

My Father's Dragon

in the Classroom

Based on the book written by
Ruth Stiles Gannett

This guide written by **Betty L. Bond**

Teacher Created Materials, Inc.
6421 Industry Way
Westminster, CA 92683
www.teachercreated.com
©2002 Teacher Created Materials
Reprinted, 2004
Made in U.S.A.
ISBN 0-7439-3157-2

Edited by
Lorin Klistoff, M.A.

Illustrated by
Kevin Barnes

Cover Art by
Brenda DiAntonis

le of Contents

Introduction

A good book can touch our lives like a good friend. Within its pages are words and characters that can inspire us to achieve our highest ideals. We can turn to it for companionship, recreation, comfort, and guidance. It can also give us a cherished story to hold in our hearts forever.

In Literature Units, great care has been taken to select books that are sure to become good friends. Teachers who use this literature unit will find that it is standards-based in literature and that it can easily be adapted for use in differentiated learning strategies. The activities presented in this literature unit can be embellished with books and supplies for use at a center for students. Teachers who use this literature unit will find the following features to supplement their own valuable ideas

- Sample Lesson Plan

- Pre-reading Activities

- Biographical Sketch and Picture of Author

- A Book Summary

- Vocabulary Lists and Suggested Vocabulary Activities

- Chapters grouped for study with each section including:

  —*quizzes*

  —*hands-on projects*

  —*cooperative learning activities*

  —*cross-curricular connections*

  —*extension into the reader's own life*

- Post-reading Activities

- Book Report Ideas

- Research Ideas

- Culminating Activities

- Options for Unit Tests

- Bibliography of Related Reading

- Answer Key

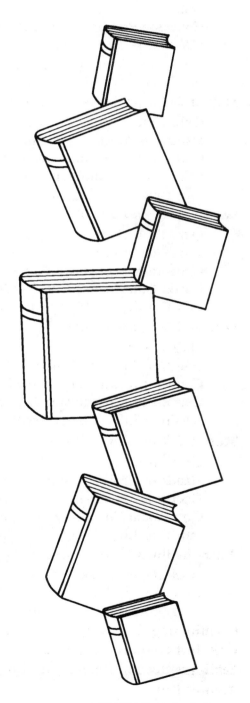

We are confident that this unit will be a valuable addition to your lesson planning. As you use our ideas, your students will learn to treasure the books to which you introduce them.

Sample Lesson Plan

Each of the lessons suggested below can take from one to several days to complete.

Lesson 1
- Introduce and complete some of the pre-reading activities (page 5).
- Read About the Author with your students (page 6).
- Write predictions in the Reading Response Journals (page 10).
- Introduce the vocabulary list for Section 1 (page 8).

Lesson 2
- Read Chapter 1 and 2. As you read, place the vocabulary words in the context of the story and discuss their meanings.
- Choose a vocabulary activity (page 9).
- Create a knapsack full of memories (page 12).
- Plan for a journey with a backpack (page 13).
- Locate directions using the sun (page 14).
- Write about fears and how to overcome them (page 15).
- Administer Section 1 quiz (page 11).

Lesson 3
- Make a rain forest (page 17).
- Record ways of showing responsibility (page 18).
- Read about the rain forest and begin research on the animals (pages 19 and 20).
- Create an emergency message (page 21).
- Administer Section 2 quiz (page 16).

Lesson 4
- Grow some ferns (page 23).
- Read situations from the book and decide whether they are fact or fiction (page 24).
- Explore Elmer's point of view with "The Hot Seat" (page 25).
- Write a message to Elmer's mother and put it in a bottle (page 26).
- Administer Section 3 quiz (page 22).

Lesson 5
- Use a magnifying glass to find an insect to write about (page 28).
- Create a travel brochure to attract people to Wild Island (page 29).
- Write sentences using alliteration (page 30).
- Construct a pop-up book (page 31).
- Administer Section 4 quiz (page 27).

Lesson 6
- Make a three-dimensional map of Wild Island (page 33).
- Discuss Elmer's choices (page 34).
- Complete the math activity (page 35).
- Compare yourself to Elmer (page 36).
- Administer Section 5 quiz (page 32).

Lesson 7
- Choose an After the Book activity (pages 37–39).
- Choose a culminating activity (pages 40–42).
- Select a test option (pages 43–45).

Before the Book

Before you begin reading *My Father's Dragon* with your students, do some pre-reading activities to stimulate interest and enhance comprehension. Here are some activities that might work well in your class.

1. Before you begin the book, review the parts of a book by discussing the title, author, table of contents, cover page, dedication page, kind of media used for the illustrations, and the About the Author and book summary on pages 6 and 7.

2. Predict what the story might be about just by looking at the cover illustration.

3. Set the stage for reading the book by talking and sharing ideas about the following:
   - Find other islands on a world map.
   - Discover what these islands have in common and create a survey of students who have been to other islands.
   - Spend time sharing experiences.

4. Develop a KWL chart asking the students what they know about exploration. The chart should reflect their prior *knowledge* (K), *what* they would like to know about exploration (W), and after the information has been collected and shared, what they *learned* (L) about exploration from the story.

5. Assign animals represented in the book for students to report on. Follow guidelines for organizing and reporting of information. These reports should be brief enough to give a short oral report of their respective animals at the appropriate chapter. (You may even be able to assign some other students to research the kinds of trees highlighted in the book.)

6. Answer the following questions:
   - Are you interested in stories about courageous children?
   - Are you interested in stories about children who overcome obstacles?
   - Are you interested in stories in which a character's creativity sparks your own creativity?
   - Would you ever be able to persevere in a hopeless situation?
   - Would you ever learn to live off nature, including the sea?
   - Would you ever face the dark alone?

7. If you became separated from your parents in an emergency situation, how would you feel? Describe how you would cope with your feelings to survive.

8. Work in a group or as a class to create stories of survival either on an isolated island or alone on an abandoned island with many unknowns beyond the trees and jungle.

9. Many students take trips with their families. They may have visited relatives and/or friends for holidays or just journeys to exciting places. Have students think about a trip they have taken with their families. Have them answer the following questions:
   - To what place did you travel with your family?
   - How did you get there?
   - Had anyone in your family ever visited this place before?
   - What new things did you learn on your trip?
   - Would you like to travel to this place again? Why or why not?
   - Where would you like to go on your next family trip? Why?

About the Author

Ruth Stiles Gannet was born in 1923 in New York City. As a child, she spent most of her summers in Connecticut where she would write in her notebooks only because she entertained herself and because . . . it was fun. She remembers the times, when, as a child growing up, she and her friends would delight in building houses and animals which she says are still there. Ruth Gannett later left New York City to attend a Quaker school in Pennsylvania, followed by Vassar College and then worked at Massachusetts Institute of Technology. While looking for a job and staying at her father's house, *My Father's Dragon* was "born" on those cold, rainy days back in Connecticut to help pass the time. Ruth had no idea of publishing it until she read it many years later to her family of seven daughters who delighted in the little boy's adventures.

Ruth wrote two sequels to *My Father's Dragon*: *Elmer and the Dragon*, and subsequently, *The Dragons of Blueland*. Mrs. Gannett is now retired and living in New York State where she is able to pursue her hobbies of spinning and dyeing. Her daughters are all grown except the youngest one, who is in high school. Mrs. Gannett also serves on the local school board where she continues to encourage students to enjoy learning.

My Father's Dragon was illustrated by Ruth's stepmother, Ruth Chrisman Gannett. It took first place in a book festival in 1948 and in 1949. It was a Newbery Honor Book. *My Father's Dragon* has been translated into Japanese, Danish, and Swedish. The author has since written two more books, *Katie and the Sad Noise* and *The Wonderful House-Boat-Train*.

My Father's Dragon

By Ruth Stiles Gannett

(Random House Children's Pub., 1987)

(Available in Canada, Random House; UK, Random Century House; AUS, Random House)

My Father's Dragon is the delightful story of a little boy, Elmer Elevator, who is led by a very persuasive cat to a wild island teeming with an emotional mixture of animals. Elmer meets the old alley cat on his street and they become good friends. The cat helps Elmer to fulfill his dream of flying by encouraging Elmer to rescue a very unhappy flying baby dragon that fell out of a cloud and onto Wild Island. The dragon was captured, tied to a pole, and ordered to serve the animals on the island as a flying ferry across a wild and treacherous river.

Elmer and the cat carefully plan the transportation and needed supplies for the rescue. The cat states he is too old to make the trip, so Elmer attempts the trip alone. He hides in a grain bag aboard a ship that will take him to the nearest place to Wild Island, the Island of Tangerina. When he arrives, he gathers tangerines for his food. He then waits till night to journey across the rocks that join both islands, fearing the possibility of dangerous animals catching him if he traveled during the day.

Upon arrival, Elmer tries to keep himself from being found but ends up meeting various animals such as a mouse, boars, tortoises, a lion, etc. With Elmer's daring streak, combined with cleverness, humor, and a most unusual backpack laden with an array of supplies, he tricks the wild beasts roaming Wild Island while on his journey to find the baby dragon and set him free. Each time Elmer reaches into his backpack, the reader is continually amused with the way in which the wild animal is tricked out of eating this adventurous, but determined, boy. For example, Elmer meets a lion that is upset about his messy mane. Elmer gives the lion a comb, a brush, and some ribbons. The lion is so preoccupied with grooming his mane that Elmer is able to make a quick escape.

After all the ingenious escapes from the wild beasts, Elmer cuts the rope and frees the dragon. They fly off together to the Island of Tangerina.

Vocabulary Lists

On this page are vocabulary lists that correspond to each sectional groupings of chapters, as outlined in the Table of Contents on page 2. Vocabulary activity ideas can be found on page 9 of this book. Vocabulary knowledge may be evaluated by including selected words in the quizzes and tests. This can be done with matching, multiple choice, or fill-in-the-blank questions.

Section 1 (*Chapters 1–2*)

obliged	patient
dependable	gangplank
inhabited	complain
inconvenient	distract
weep	miserable
dock	knapsack

Section 2 (*Chapters 3–4*)

cargo	rumbling
merchant	gloomy
extraordinary	compass
trundled	solemn
punctual	unreliable
slippery	scarce

Section 3 (*Chapters 5–6*)

familiar	squirm
palm trees	suspicious
craving	mahogany
trespassing	dense
frantically	contradict
soared	clearing

Section 4 (*Chapters 7–8*)

peered	magnifying
forelock	dignified
mangroves	banyan tree
glaring	fierce
frantically	enormous
mane	miraculous

Section 5 (*Chapters 9–10*)

summon	seething
conduct	irate
craving	screeching
peeping	soared
delicious	somersault
furious	grinning

Vocabulary Activity Ideas

Completing some vocabulary activities based on the words in the book will help your students learn and retain the words. A list of vocabulary words is provided for each section of the book. You may wish to divide these words into smaller groups for students. The groups may define the words, find them in the context of the book, and present the information to the class to record in a vocabulary notebook.

The students may work in small groups or individually in order to study the words. Here are a few ideas for activities to try with the vocabulary words in *My Father's Dragon*.

Spelling/Vocabulary Baseball

Divide your class into two teams and set up a baseball diamond with a soft ball that can be thrown in the classroom. The batter either spells a vocabulary word or says the definition of the vocabulary word given to them by the pitcher. If the batter answers correctly, the pitcher throws the ball. The batter uses his or her hand as a bat. Switch teams when there are three outs.

Vocabulary Bee

Follow the pattern of a traditional spelling bee to conduct a Vocabulary Bee. Challenge students to give the correct definition of the word as well as the correct spelling. Have students find the root word for each vocabulary word. They may then create new words by adding prefixes or suffixes to the root word. Have a contest to see who can discover the most new words.

Illustrated Dictionary

As a group activity, have students work together to create an illustrated dictionary of the animals, trees, and rich action verbs presented in the book.

Pictionary Vocabulary

This is modeled after the popular game, Pictionary. In this game, students are divided into two teams. A team is chosen to start the game. Each player chooses a vocabulary word card prepared by the teacher. They pick a card and try to draw it so their team can guess what it is before the time of one or two minutes is up. If the playing team guesses the word within the time limit, a point is given, and the same team continues until they can't guess the correct word within the time limit. The opposing team then follows the same procedure. The winning team is the team with the most points. The length of play can be determined by the teacher.

Travel Brochure

Pretend you are an advertising person for the Island of Tangerina and Wild Island. You are interested in attracting tourists. Make a travel brochure for your area using the vocabulary words. Describe the trip in exciting and colorful ways. Anything in the setting or story itself, such as landscape or activities, may be included.

Parts of Speech

Have each cooperative learning team sort the vocabulary words into piles by their parts of speech. For example, nouns can be placed in one pile and verbs in another pile. Use these words as an introduction to a new part of your English textbook.

Reading Response Journals

One great way to ensure that the reading of *My Father's Dragon* becomes a personal experience for each student is to include the use of reading response journals in your plans. In these journals, students can be encouraged to respond to the story in a number of ways. Since Elmer follows a precise journey, with very special circumstances, students can write their predictions of how he solves his problems, and compare them to the way Elmer does.

The following are suggestions for using reading response journals:

1. Tell students that the purpose of their journal is to record their thoughts, ideas, observations, and questions as they read *My Father's Dragon*.

2. Provide students with (or ask them to suggest) topics from the story about which it would be interesting for them to write. Here are some examples from the chapters in Section 1.

   - Looking at the cover, ask the children to predict what the story is about. Remind them that they are welcome to change their predictions as they read. Give them the opportunity to share among their groups or classmates.

   - At the end of chapter one, ask students to predict what they think the cat saw that made him want to weep.

   - On a piece of large chart paper, write the description of the baby dragon as described by the cat. Read the passage to the students. Tell them that they will have two minutes to read and remember it. Take the description away and ask students to draw as much as they can remember and to keep their version to themselves. Allow approximately 15 minutes, then ask them to share. Note the differences among the other students' versions. Later, when they have seen the illustrator's picture, point out that sometimes their imaginations and mind pictures are different and sometimes even better. (Make sure you do this before they read and see the illustration of the dragon.)

3. Give students quotes from the novel and ask them to write their own responses. (Make sure that you do this before you go over the quotations in class.) In groups, they could list different responses to the same quote.

   Allow your students time to write in their journals daily. Personal reflections can be read by the teacher, but no corrections or letter grades should be assigned. Credit should be given for effort, and all of the students who sincerely try should be awarded credit. If a grade is desired, grade according to the number of entries.

10

Quiz Time

Directions: Please answer the questions below.

1. On the back of this paper, sequence three important events that happened to Elmer Elevator before he left on his journey.

2. Where did Elmer and the cat meet?

_____

3. How did Elmer's mother feel about Elmer bringing a stray cat home and feeding it?

_____

_____

4. What did Elmer tell the cat he wanted to do more than anything?

_____

5. Name the two islands about which the cat told Elmer.

_____

6. The cat described the animals on the island. What was their big problem?

_____

_____

7. Explain how the animals were going to get to the other side of the river.

_____

8. How did the baby dragon get to the island with the animals?

_____

9. Write three items that Elmer had in his knapsack.

_____

10. How do you feel about how the animals treated the baby dragon? Why?

_____

Knapsack Full of Memories

Elmer and the cat packed some very useful items into Elmer's knapsack before he left for Wild Island. Although Elmer faced numerous dangers during the day, we never read what he did at night, alone, in the jungle, on an island inhabited by wild animals. Perhaps he thought of his warm bed at home, sitting down to dinner with his family, or some other family event.

Memories are an important part of all of our lives. We all have special memories of past events which create a positive, lasting place in our minds which we might think about in more lonely times or when we are away from familiar surroundings. Try to think of some of those memories and write them down in a short paragraph. Obtain a regular knapsack or bag and place your paragraph memories in it.

You may want to include some of the following items in your knapsack:

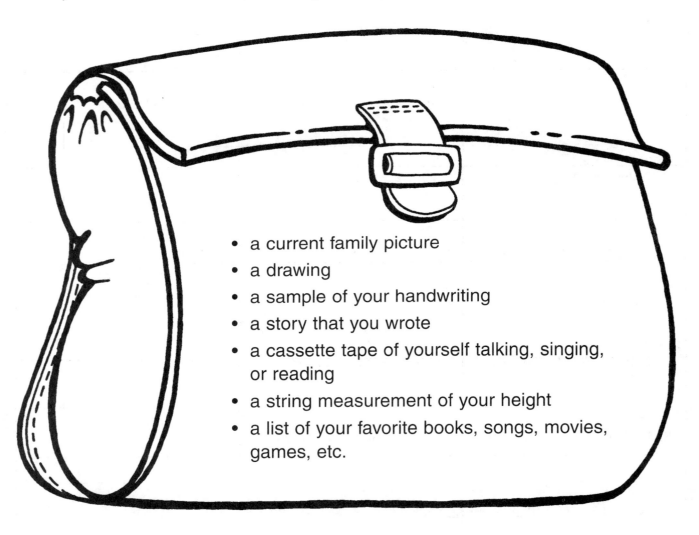

- a current family picture
- a drawing
- a sample of your handwriting
- a story that you wrote
- a cassette tape of yourself talking, singing, or reading
- a string measurement of your height
- a list of your favorite books, songs, movies, games, etc.

Once you have gathered your memories, place them in your knapsack and close it. Keep your knapsack in a safe place and open it some time in the future. You might be surprised by what you learn when you look back on your memories.

Packing for a Journey

Elmer took his father's knapsack and packed very interesting items to take with him on his journey. Imagine that your group is going to an island for a certain amount of time. List the items that Elmer took. Then think about the things that your group could take with them. List the items and then explain why your group would take each item.

Elmer's Items	Your Group's Items	Explanation

Locating Directions by the Sun

Elmer landed on the Island of Tangerina and crossed the Ocean Rocks to Wild Island. Elmer may have used the sun to help him find his direction.

The sun provides us with constant directional source and is, therefore, a natural compass. Work in teams to try some of the following methods of locating north, south, east, and west with the use of the sun. Check your results with a compass. When you are finished, make notes about which ways are most accurate. Share your results with the class.

1. **Sun:** The sun rises in the east and sets in the west. Try observing the sun and locating north, south, east, and west. (This method will be more accurate early or late in the day when the sun is not straight overhead.)

2. **Watch:** If you have a watch that is set to the local time, you can use it as a compass. Hold the watch flat in your hand and then turn the watch until the hour hand is pointing to the sun. If you draw an imaginary line between the hour hand and 12:00, the line will be pointing south.

3. **Stick Shadow:** You will need a flat, sandy location and a short, straight stick for this method. (A craft stick would work well.) Push the stick into the ground, angling it toward the sun, so that it will not make a shadow. Wait until it forms a shadow at least 7" (18 cm) long. The shadow that the stick makes will be pointing east. Now you can locate north, south, and west.

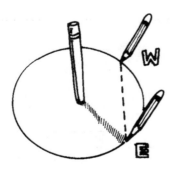

4. **Equal Length Shadow:** You will need a flat, sandy location, two pencils, a yardstick, and a piece of string. In the morning, push the yardstick into the ground. Tie the string with a loose knot at the bottom of the yardstick. Stretch the string out from the yardstick to the end of the yardstick's shadow. Tie the pencil to the string at this point. Use the pencil to sketch a circle in the dirt around the yardstick and then push the pencil into the ground where the shadow meets the circle. In the afternoon, take the second pencil and push it into the ground where the new shadow meets the circle. Sketch a straight line in the dirt to connect the two pencils. This line marks east and west. The morning marker is west. Now you can find north and south.

Fear

In this part of the story, Elmer packs up, with the help of the cat and leaves on a ship. He hides in the hold for six days and nights, fearing his capture and return home. Thus, many times in our story, Elmer faces his fears in many dangerous situations.

Most people have a slight fear of something, such as spiders, heights, or thunderstorms. These fears are often in response to experiences someone has had in the past, such as walking through a spider web, falling from a loft, or being caught outside in a storm. Although it may seem silly at times to be afraid of something, fear is very real and facing one's fears can be very difficult.

Think of a few things of which you or someone you know are afraid. List them below. Then brainstorm ideas about what can be done to overcome those fears. When you are finished, choose a partner and take turns role-playing one of the fear scenarios and solutions.

Fear	How It Can Be Overcome

Quiz Time

1. On the back of this paper, list three major events that happened in this section.

2. Where did Elmer hide on the ship? How did he hide himself?

   _____

3. When the merchant felt the bags of wheat, he almost found Elmer. What did the merchant think he felt in the bag?

   _____

4. Elmer woke up hungry the next morning on a sandy beach. What did he discover above his head?

   _____

5. As Elmer crossed the rocks from Tangerina to Wild Island, he stepped on something very strange. What was it that made a very loud noise?

   _____

6. What kind of animal did Elmer first meet after he arrived on Wild Island?

   _____

7. What did the animal think about Elmer's knapsack?

   _____

8. There were two scary things that happened to Elmer. The first scary thing was telling the tortoises about what was on his back. Tell about the second scary thing that happened to Elmer.

   _____

9. One of the animals said there were three signs of invasion. What were they?

   _____

   _____

10. Elmer was taught a lesson. What did he learn at this point in the story?

   _____

Rain Forest

In this part of the story, Elmer walks through a jungle or rain forest with beautiful trees and very interesting animals. It is often difficult for students to realize the size of a rain forest from books or activities. Here is an activity that gives some idea about size proportion to your students.

Setting the Stage

Discuss with the class the concept of size. How big do they think the trees in the rain forest are? as big as a large building? What things might be in a rain forest?

Materials

- assorted books on the rain forest

- construction paper—assorted colors

- scissors, glue, crayons, markers

- long sheets of brown butcher paper—enough to construct a floor-to-ceiling tree

- green butcher paper to construct palm-like leaves

Procedure

1. Have students research plants and animals that live in the rain forest.

2. With students working in teams, have the teams draw, color, and cut out a variety of plants and animals that are found in the rain forest.

3. While the students are constructing the wildlife, twist long sheets of brown butcher paper into the trunk and branches of a tree. Ambitious teachers can construct more than one to give the feeling of the understory and canopy.

4. Mount the trunk and branches of the tree to the ceiling and walls in a corner of the room. Have the branches extend over the students' desks to reconstruct the feeling of the rain forest.

5. Cut the giant palm fronds, banana leaves, or leaves of other rain forest trees and attach them to the branches. Make sure they hang down over your students.

6. After the students have completed their animals and plants, arrange them in the layers of the rain forest in which you would find them.

7. If floor space allows, spread some burlap or blankets on the floor to represent the ground in the rain forest.

Extension

- The rain forest makes a wonderful reading corner for the students. It can be left up all year.

- In the rain forest journal, have your students write for young children, three to six years old, a story about an adventure in a rain forest.

Be Responsible!

Setting the Stage

Discuss with students how Elmer showed a strong sense of responsibility as he endured the swamps, animals, and jungle to rescue the baby dragon. He was determined to fulfill his promise to the cat. Tell them how Elmer remembered things the cat told him, keeping his calm throughout the ordeal.

Procedure

1. Start a class discussion on the important topic of responsibility and how the students have shown responsibility in their own lives. Record the students' responses on chart or butcher paper.

2. Give each student the form below to keep a week's record of the ways he or she showed responsibility at home, with friends, or in his or her own neighborhood or community.

3. At the end of a week, pair the students to share their own charts.

Days of the Week	How I Showed Responsibility
Monday	
Tuesday	
Wednesday	
Thursday	
Friday	
Saturday	
Sunday	

Nature Notes

Elmer Elevator met many wild animals on his journey through Wild Island. There is an extraordinary number of different animals living in the rain forest for their food, shelter, and protection. In fact, many of the jungle plants depend upon these animals for pollination, seed dispersal, and even protection. The bats, for example, obtain nectar from flowers for their food. At the same time, they are helping to pollinate that same plant. The relationship where one species helps another to survive is called *mutualism*.

Animal species in the rain forest are just as diverse as the plant life. The largest group of animal life is the insects. Beetles, butterflies, spiders, centipedes, scorpions, and other arthropods make this group the most numerous and diverse group in the tropics. Many new species are being found each year to add to their numbers. Most of the insects in the rain forest are not as helpful as the ant. The anopheles mosquito is a carrier of a disease called malaria, and the tsetse fly is responsible for sleeping sickness.

Another large population of animal in the rain forest is reptiles. The largest snakes on Earth, the pythons of the Old World and the anacondas of South America, are found in the rain forest. Lizards are also abundant in the rain forest. You can see many species warming themselves in the high branches of the trees during the day. Also amphibians, such as frogs and salamanders, are tropical inhabitants.

Of all the diverse animal life found in the rain forest, the mammals are the most well known. When most people think of the jungle, they think of monkeys swinging from vines in the trees, but the tropics are home to more species of bats than any other mammal. These bats are an extremely important factor in the rain forests' continual regrowth.

Bird diversity is also abundant in the tropics. Many of these species include the most colorful of all the birds in the world. They include the parrots, macaws, birds of paradise, and even the parakeet. The jungles of South America are mainly inhabited by birds of prey such as the harpy eagle and the African crowned eagle.

Nature Notes *(cont.)*

Read the background on the rain forest on page 19. Then research three of the following animals: lions, tigers, boars, tortoises, gorillas, monkeys, or crocodiles. Use the form below to help organize your research. If you want to include some of the other animals that are also listed and are of special interest to you, ask your teacher.

After you have researched these animals, prepare a presentation to the class of the interesting facts that you have discovered. To make your presentation even more interesting, draw a picture of your animal.

Day: _____   Date: _____

Animal: _____

Common Name: _____

Scientific Name: _____

Where Seen: _____

Description: _____

_____

Predator/Prey: _____

_____

(drawing)

Creating an Emergency Message

Imagine that you have just been stranded on an island in the South Pacific. There are four of you. You have a radio that can transmit a message for help, but it has limited battery energy. If you are careful, you can transmit one ten-second message. You realize your message will be heard by rescuers, and you want these rescuers to be prepared when they arrive. In this message, you must also give your rescuers landmarks. To the east, there is a volcano. The northern end of the island is rimmed with a beach of deep, black sand, and there is a large waterfall to the south. When your ship is destroyed, you know that you were around 15° S latitude and 150° W longitude. You also know that you may have drifted west of this location due to a strong current. One member of your party has broken his leg. Another person is unconscious. Both need medical help immediately.

Create a ten-second message that will direct your rescuers to your location and will ensure that they come prepared for your emergency. Write your message below and then practice it until you can say it clearly in ten seconds.

_____

_____

_____

_____

_____

_____

_____

_____

_____

_____

_____

Quiz Time

1. On the back of this paper, sequence three important events from this part of the story.

2. Describe the problem that Elmer had going through the jungle.

   _____

3. What did Elmer take out of his knapsack to help him find his way to the river?

   _____

4. Along the way, Elmer heard some whispery voices coming from the jungle. What did he see walking toward him in the clearing?

   _____

5. Why were these animals so angry with him? _____

   _____

6. How did Elmer solve their problem? Tell what was so special about the object that Elmer gave the animals.

   _____

   _____

7. Just as he was feeling very safe, what greeted him around the next corner?

   _____

8. Elmer became very thirsty after walking for such a long time, so he stopped to wade into a little pool of water. Suddenly, he was hanging in the air. Write a sentence about this event, telling what kind of animal it was and why the animal was tossing Elmer up and down.

   _____

   _____

9. What was bothering the animal?

   _____

10. Describe how Elmer solved his problem.

    _____

    _____

Growing Ferns

In Chapter 5, Elmer was trying to follow the wide and muddy river through the dense jungle where he was stuck by ferns with sticky leaves. Ferns are a kind of plant that stay green all year long. There are 12,000 kinds of ferns. Some turn brown in their life cycle. There are other kinds of trees which have leaves that change to a different color and drop off the trees. These trees are called deciduous. Each kind of tree group has many different leaves that are very interesting when we take the time to carefully examine them. Answer the following question and you may begin growing your own ferns.

Question

Is it possible to grow ferns indoors?

Setting the Stage

- Ask students what types of plants grow in their homes. By now many of them should be well aware of the different types of plants.
- Ask students if they have any ferns growing in their yards. With parent permission, perhaps they could bring in some cuttings for the class to examine.
- Discuss with students the needs of a plant: soil, water, air, and sunlight. Have students try to determine the best way to grow plants in the classroom.

Materials

- 5-gallon (20 L) water jar
- several tiny plants (e.g., ferns, mosses, etc.)
- newspaper
- bag of potting soil
- a long stick such as yard or meter stick

(*Note to Teacher:* You may choose to have students prepare more than one terrarium.)

Procedure (Student Instruction)

1. Spread a newspaper over your desk and floor to catch any soil that may fall.
2. Fill ½ of the jar with potting soil.
3. Water the soil until it is evenly wet but the water has not puddled.
4. Carefully decide where you want your plants located. Once they are placed in the jar, you will not be able to move them easily.
5. Dig a hole with your long stick. (A yard stick or a pointer works well.)
6. Gently push the plant into the neck of the jar and use the stick to position it over the hole.
7. Pack the soil around the roots of the plant with the stick to position it over the hole.
8. Repeat the same procedure for the rest of your plants. Care must be taken not to overplant. The plants will grow to full size inside the jar.
9. Water the jar sparingly. Moisture from the soil and the plants will form on the sides of the bottle and trickle down to the soil.
10. Place the jar in the sunlight or partial shade and watch the plants grow.
11. After one week, draw a picture of what your terrarium looks like.

Extensions

- Have students research other ways of growing gardens indoors.
- Have a class discussion about hydroponics.

Closure

In their plant journals, have students keep a weekly log of how their garden grows.

Fact or Fiction?

Knowing the difference between the life of the imagination and real life is important; yet, it is often fun to enjoy imagining about fictitious things.

Below are several situations that might take place in real life or the life of the imagination. In groups of three, look at these situations and place a check in the correct column to indicate whether the situation is real (*fact*) or imaginative (*fiction*).

	Fact	Fiction
1. A cat drinks from a saucer of milk.		
2. The ship sails to the island.		
3. The rhinoceros polishes his tusk with toothpaste.		
4. Animals get their mail delivered on the island.		
5. The jungle has high ferns with sticky leaves.		
6. A baby dragon falls from a cloud into the river.		
7. A lion grooms his mane with a comb.		
8. There is a jungle on the island.		
9. A boy flies on a dragon.		
10. A whale snores.		
11. The swamp has oozy, mucky mud.		
12. Tigers like chewing gum.		
13. A rhinoceros has a private weeping pool.		
14. The boy eats tangerines.		
15. The boars talk to each other.		
16. Tigers get hungry.		
17. The rhinoceros has a tusk.		
18. The jungle is gloomy and dense.		

Choose one of these situations and write a story about it on the back of this paper. Include three parts in your story:

- the introduction of the characters and the situation,
- the event that happens to create a problem, and
- the solution to the problem that was created.

After you have proofread and rewritten your story, read it to your classmates and have them decide whether it is real or fiction.

The Hot Seat

When Elmer met some of the animals, they were frequently angry because they thought Elmer did something wrong. Elmer's mother was also upset with him for not obeying her and may have worried about his safety. Through some of the characters in the book, we learn a different side of Elmer besides the caring, gentle, little boy who took care of a cat. Think for a moment how some of them felt when they first met Elmer. From the point of view of the animals or the mother, try to think of questions that you would like to ask Elmer if he was right in your classroom. One question can be from the mother and another question can be asked from one of the animal characters. Someone can pretend to be Elmer and sit where everyone can see him or her. The student playing Elmer can call on people to ask a question and then respond from what would be Elmer's point of view. A sample question might be from the mother. "Elmer, why did you run away? I missed you so much." Elmer might respond, "Well, Mom, I was upset that you didn't let me have the cat for my pet. I promised I would take care of her."

Character: _____

Question: _____

Character: _____

Question: _____

Character: _____

Question: _____

Character: _____

Question: _____

Character: _____

Question: _____

Message in a Bottle

Elmer ran away from home without telling his mother where he was going. By this time, she may be worried about her little boy.

Pretend that you are Elmer and think about your mother worrying where you are and what you are **doing.** Use the space below to send her a message to make her feel better. You may want to tell her **about your** exciting trip on the cargo ship, or walking across a whale's back, or meeting up with some **very funny** animals. After you finish writing, cut out the letter and roll it up. Place the rolled paper **inside a** bottle. Create an address for Mrs. Elevator and send it.

Extensions

- Draw a colored picture of the places where you were or what you look like and put it in the bottle.
- Write a message to the cat, letting her know how you are doing and where you are on your **journey** to rescue the baby dragon.
- Write a message describing the jungle with the swamp, the wide and muddy river, and the thick, **dense** trees.

Quiz Time

1. On the back of this paper, list three important events that happened in this part of the story.

2. As Elmer walked through the jungle, he met another animal. What was it? What was it doing?

   _____

3. This animal was upset about something. Describe the problem.

   _____

4. Again, Elmer Elevator solved the animal's problem with something from his knapsack. Tell what Elmer used from his supplies. How did Elmer escape harm from this animal?

   _____

   _____

5. When Elmer stopped to read the signs at the crossroads, he saw something. What was it?

   _____

6. Because Elmer was so tired, he stopped to rest under a palm tree. Suddenly, a big, black thing popped out. Describe what it was.

   _____

7. This big, black thing was raging. Tell about the problem of this animal.

   _____

8. This animal did something strange. Describe what fell out of the palm tree that tried to help the animal.

   _____

9. Elmer reached into his knapsack again to help this poor animal. What did Elmer take out and for what was it used?

   _____

   _____

10. Why do you think Elmer was able to get away and continue his journey to rescue the dragon?

   _____

   _____

Magnify This!

When Elmer took out the magnifying glasses for the monkeys to find the fleas on the gorilla, they were shocked to find hundreds of them! A magnifying glass enables us to see tiny things close up.

Get with a partner and explore grass areas. Try to find some tiny insects. Sketch a picture of one insect in detail. Then write a paragraph about the insect using descriptive language. For example, "As I looked through the lens, I couldn't believe what I saw. It had eight hairy legs, a striped body, and . . ."

_____

_____

_____

_____

_____

_____

_____

Travel Brochure

The island provided Elmer Elevator with challenges that were met by his clever wit and well-supplied knapsack. He saw and experienced a world that he had never before seen. Imagine what Elmer might have told everyone in his town about the island.

Many people like to travel to islands and read travel brochures for recreational activities and places to stay and eat. For this activity, you will be working in small groups to create a travel brochure for Wild Island. From the suggested list below, choose a section that seems interesting to you and other members of your group, then present it to the class. Remember, you might think of other things to do and places to stay on Wild Island to include in your brochure. Be sure to include prices and information about the activities as well as any special equipment, including clothing that may be needed.

Plants	Animals	Land Features	Activities	Lodging
palm trees	tortoises	swamp	snorkeling	hotels
mahogany trees	boars	river	deep sea diving	tree houses
banyan trees	tigers	jungle	water skiing	beach bungalows
ferns	rhinoceroses	beach	hang gliding	thatched huts
wahoo bush	gorillas	ocean	swimming	over-water bungalows
tall grass	crocodiles	ocean rocks	hiking	

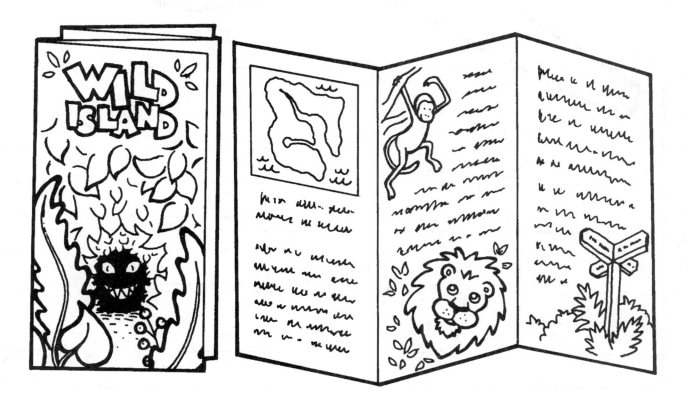

Alliteration Amusement

In Chapter 8, "My Father Meets a Gorilla," the gorilla summoned the monkeys to help him find his fleas. Their names were Rosie, Rhoda, Rachel, Ruthie, Ruby, and Roberta. All names begin with the letter R. This style of writing is known as alliteration. Most of the letters of a phrase or sentence begin with the same first letter, adding some interest to the piece of writing.

In the boxes below, write sentences where most of the words begin with the same first letter. For example, "Betty bakes beautiful beans in Boston while blowing big balloons."

Characters Popping Up!

Elmer is quite a character. In the beginning, he showed that he was gentle and caring. In the middle, we discovered that he was clever, smart, helpful, and frequently brave. He traveled alone to a wild island teeming with dangerous animals!

Try to find an interest or a quality you have that is similar to Elmer. Write a complete sentence about it. For example, you may think that you like to travel or that you are caring when you take care of your pets. Create a character pop-up book and compare yourself to Elmer.

Materials

- white construction paper
- colored pencils or markers
- crayons
- glue
- scissors

Directions

1. Have students fold a piece of construction paper in half. Cut slits down from the fold.

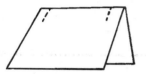

2. Help students push the cut area through the fold and crease it to form a pop-up section. (*Note*: Students can also make a pop-up section by folding a sheet of paper in fourths lengthwise and taping the top and bottom of the paper together to make a rectangular box. Glue the box to the pop-up page.)

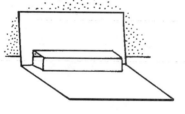

4. Help students write sentences above the pop-up section and glue the appropriate drawing to the pop-up page.

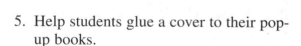

5. Help students glue a cover to their pop-up books.

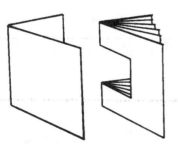

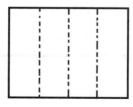 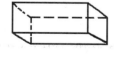

3. Have students make other pop-up pages and glue them back to back.

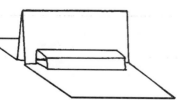

Quiz Time

1. On the back of this paper, sequence three important events that happened in this part of the story.

2. Elmer saw a sign on a flagpole giving directions to call for the dragon. He was worried about following the sign's directions. Why was that?

   _____

3. Another animal came up to Elmer. Tell what kind of animal it was and why it wanted Elmer.

   _____

4. Describe how Elmer solved this animal's problem. Tell what Elmer took from his knapsack this time.

   _____

5. Write two sentences telling how Elmer tried to get to the other side of the river.

   _____

   _____

6. Just as Elmer was about to step over to the other side of the river, what did he see behind him?

   _____

   _____

7. The baby dragon was very excited to see Elmer. What did Elmer use to free the dragon?

   _____

8. The author tells about a very funny scene with the animals on the backs of crocodiles. What was this scene? How did the crocodiles feel about this?

   _____

   _____

9. Elmer quickly climbed onto the back of the baby dragon. Where did the pair go?

   _____

   _____

10. At the end of the story, the baby dragon and Elmer fly away together. If you were Elmer, where would you want the baby dragon to take you?

   _____

   _____

Three-Dimensional Map

In the story, *My Father's Dragon*, Ruth S. Gannett describes all the different land forms of this island, such as the swamp, the jungle, the wide and muddy river, the coast, and the big and small clearings.

Work with a partner to make your own three-dimensional map showing the features on Wild Island. Use the map at the end of the story along with the text to help you fill the shape. Then design your three-dimensional map.

Materials

- a piece of heavy cardboard
- paint
- stove or hot plate (*for teacher use*)
- pot for mixing dough
- food coloring

Playdough Ingredients

- 1 cup (250 mL) of flour
- ½ cup (125 mL) salt
- 1 tablespoon (15 mL) cream of tartar
- 1 tablespoon (15 mL) oil
- 1 cup (250 mL) water

Directions

1. Mix dry ingredients with the oil. Add water. With adult supervision, cook over medium heat, stirring constantly until dough is stiff. Take dough out of pot, allow to cool so you can handle it, and knead until it has the consistency of playdough. If you want to add food coloring instead of painting the final product, you can color your dough as it is cooking. (*Note*: The dough can be made in advance and packaged in airtight plastic bags for later use.)

2. Spread the dough on the cardboard to form your map.

3. Shape mountains and valleys on the flat surface by molding the dough. You can also add trees, rocks, or other landmarks while the dough is still soft.

4. When it is dry, you can paint the surface to look like your landscape.

5. Add signs indicating places or events in the book. You can also add models of the characters to the surface.

Go to Your Corners!

In this section of the book, Elmer must think of a way to get across the river. He walks back and forth trying to think of the best way to get to the baby dragon. According to his choices, he can do any of them, but they all have a consequence. His choices are the following:

- Call to the dragon to cross the river.
- Climb the pole and cross on the rope.
- Swim across the river.

Setup

1. Print the choices listed above on sentence strips or construction paper.

2. Place tape on the back and display each choice in one of three corners of the room.

Procedure

1. Read and discuss each one of Elmer's choices, evaluating the consequences.

2. Have students think and decide what they would do if they were Elmer with these problems. Ask them to keep their opinions secret from their classmates.

3. Provide simple guidelines for movement and talk.

4. After a signal from the teacher, ask students to move to a corner of the room where there is a label stating their choice.

5. When students arrive at their destinations, tell them to talk among their classmates about why that choice is the best choice.

6. Have students record their reasons on paper.

7. Have students choose a person who will speak for the entire group. He or she will explain the choice and the reasons to the rest of the class.

8. Ask for verbal explanations from each "corner" of the room.

9. When each group has shared its reasons, read chapter nine aloud. Ask students to compare their choices with Elmer's by writing in their reading response journals.

Animal Math

In this part of the story, Elmer walks across the crocodiles' backs to the other side. Just as he arrives on the opposite bank, he sees the other animals in pursuit. There were seven tigers, one rhinoceros, two lions, one gorilla, six monkeys, and two boars along with the seventeen very hungry crocodiles. Solve the following story problems using the animals previously mentioned.

1. Using the list and number of animals previously mentioned, add the total number of animals on the backs of the crocodiles behind Elmer. _____

2. If one crocodile weighs 1,125 pounds, how much will 9 crocodiles weigh? _____

3. One tiger weighs 250 pounds. What is the total weight of four tigers? _____

4. If the gorilla weighs 356 pounds and the rhinoceros weighs 2,160 pounds, what is their total weight? _____

5. One of the crocodiles has a lion and a monkey on his back. The lion weighs 300 pounds and the monkey weighs 55 pounds. How much weight is on the crocodile's back? _____

6. A lion can live for 24 years. A rhinoceros can live for 16 more years than a lion. How old can a rhinoceros live to be? _____

7. Each of the 6 monkeys has 4 legs. How many legs are on the 6 monkeys altogether? _____

8. If each of the 17 crocodiles is 12 feet long and they are stretched end to end across the wide and muddy river, how wide is the river? _____

9. Elmer packed two-dozen pink lollipops. If he gave 17 of them to the crocodiles, how many did he have left? _____

10. Elmer braided the lion's forelock, containing 21 strands of hair. If he divided them into groups of three, how many braids were formed in the lion's forelock? _____

Two Sides of Elmer

Elmer was very kind to the old alley cat at the beginning of the story, but there were two sides of Elmer. Oftentimes, Elmer helped the animals with their problems; while at other times, he made them upset. In the beginning of the story, Elmer also ran away without telling his mother.

Activity A

In the chart below, write some responses in the "positive" side that tell about the good traits of Elmer, using evidence from the book. On the "negative" side, also using evidence, write some traits that he needed to try to improve.

Positive	Negative

Activity B

Now, think about yourself. Maybe there are some qualities that you like about yourself. Write them in the "positive" side, using evidence from your life. Sometimes, there are qualities that we would like to improve. Write these down as well. Share the results with a partner, if you wish.

Positive	Negative

Book Report Ideas

There are many ways to report on a book once you have read it. After you have finished reading *My Father's Dragon*, choose one method of reporting on the book. It may be an idea your teacher suggests, an idea of your own, or one of the ways mentioned below.

Book Character

This report requires creativity and imagination. Choose one animal character from the book. Dress up as the animal. Tell the animal's point of view.

Into the Future

In this report, you will predict what really happened to all the animals on Wild Island after Elmer and the baby dragon flew away. It may take the form of a story, a narrative, or drama.

Read All About It!

Elmer is a hero for rescuing the baby dragon. Design a newspaper headline with an article about the daring rescue.

Literature Interview

This report is done in pairs. One student will pretend to be Elmer and steep himself completely in this persona. The other student will play the role of a radio or television interviewer, trying to provide the audience with insights into the character's personality and life that the audience most wants to know. It is the responsibility of the partners to create meaningful questions and appropriate answers. You may want to tape the interview for other classmates.

Travel Brochure

Design a travel brochure for Wild Island as a place for an adventure. Include actual scenes from the book as well as places of interest and exciting things to do. Your job is to make it a great place for tourists.

Twenty Questions

After the class finishes the book, each student wears a sign labeled with the name of a character from the book on his or her back. Provide students with 20 slips of paper with his or her initials on each one. The students may move about the room and ask "yes" or "no" questions about their character. They may not ask direct questions like, "Am I a mouse?" if there is only one mouse in the story. For each question, they must give away a slip of paper. At the end of the 20 questions, each one can guess which character he or she was. You may shorten the questions to ten or less to fit the situation.

Come to Life!

This report is one that lends itself to a group project. A size-appropriate group prepares a scene from the story for dramatization, acts it out, and relates the significance of the scene to the entire book. Costumes, props, and sound effects will add to the dramatization.

Research Ideas

Describe three things you read in *My Father's Dragon* about which you would like to learn more.

1. _____

   _____

2. _____

   _____

3. _____

   _____

As you read *My Father's Dragon*, you encountered many images of animals, habitat, geography, and ways of coping. To increase your understanding of the characters and events of the book, research to find out more about these animals, places, and things.

Work in a group to research one or more of the topics you named above or topics that are listed below. Share your findings with the rest of the class in any appropriate form of presentation.

islands	tigers
rivers	lions
mahogany trees	rhinoceros
palm trees	gorillas
banyan trees	primates
tangerine trees	crocodiles
cargo ships	alligators
dinosaurs	tortoise
dragons	turtles
explorers	boars

Any Questions?

When you finished reading *My Father's Dragon*, did you have any questions that were left unanswered? If so, write them on the lines below.

_____

_____

_____

_____

_____

_____

_____

Next, work in a group or by yourself to prepare possible answers for some or all of the questions you wrote above and those written below. When you have finished your predictions, share your ideas with the rest of the class.

- Describe how the dragon felt when Elmer cut the rope.

- Will the baby dragon be happier now that he is with Elmer?

- Where will Elmer and baby dragon go after the Island of Tangerina?

- What will Elmer's mother think if he comes home with the baby dragon?

- Who will take care of the baby dragon if he is injured?

- How do you think Elmer feels now that he is able to fly?

- How will the animals get people and mail across the island now?

- If the baby dragon wants to travel alone or go back to his cloud, will Elmer let the dragon go?

- What would have happened to Elmer if all the animals made it across the river?

- Do you think the alley cat would want to fly with Elmer and the baby dragon? If so, where would she want to go?

Three-Dimensional Diorama

Cooperative groups of two or four can work together to build a diorama of Wild Island. First, they should decide on which part of the island they will work to complete the project. Then, they need to gather their materials and follow the directions below.

Materials

- corrugated cardboard cut in 10-inch (25-cm) squares
- tagboard or poster board
- marking pens
- tempera paint and paintbrush
- scissors
- glue
- old travel and/or nature magazines

Directions

1. Make as many tagboard squares with tabs as you will need. (See diagram below.)

2. On one side of each square, draw a picture or cut out pictures from magazines and glue to the squares. Make sure the drawings or pictures are related to the story.

3. On the back of each square, write a sentence or two about the plant or animal that Elmer met as he traveled through Wild Island.

4. Draw the shape of Wild Island on the cardboard, and paint. Allow time to dry.

5. Cut slits in the base and slide the tabs into the slits. Be careful to face all the pictures in the same direction.

6. Students can share their completed projects within small groups. Then continue to switch groups until everyone has seen all the projects.

Extensions

- Write clues or a question on one side of the tagboard squares. Then write answers on the opposite side. Pictures can be drawn on the front or back.

- Students can construct three-dimensional dioramas to show some things they like to do at the ocean (swim, surf, sail, fish) or to demonstrate what they like to see at the ocean (seashells, waves, sandcastles).

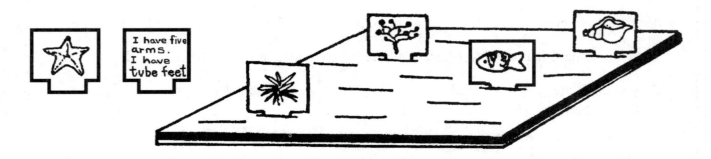

Write Your Own Sequel

Elmer successfully rescues the baby dragon. He climbs onto the dragon and they fly off together to the shores of Tangerina! We do not know where the dragon takes Elmer.

Write the sequel and decide where they go and what events happen along the way. All good stories have a beginning, middle, and end. Use the form below to help you organize your story. You may want to draw pictures of the events and then publish your story for others to enjoy in your classroom or other places outside the classroom!

Beginning (Setting): _____

_____

_____

Characters: _____

_____

Middle

    Event 1: _____

    _____

    Event 2: _____

    _____

    Event 3: _____

    _____

End: _____

_____

_____

_____

Accordion Booklet

Many interesting events took place in *My Father's Dragon*. One of the ways to remember these events is to record them with a drawing in an accordion booklet. Working with a partner, discuss the major events in several or all of the chapters in the book. Using the booklets below, draw and color the main event in each of the chapters. Indicate the chapter number you are illustrating, using short titles to explain your artwork.

When your drawing is complete, cut out the strips and tape them together. Carefully fold the booklet back and forth, accordion-style, along the dotted lines.

| *My Father's Dragon*

by

Ruth Stiles Gannet | Chapter _____

_____ | Chapter _____

_____ |

| Chapter _____

_____ | Chapter _____

_____ | Chapter _____

_____ |

Sequence the Story!

Put the following events in order as they occurred in the story by numbering them 1–15.

_____ Elmer walks across the rocks from the Isle of Tangerina to Wild Island.

_____ The alley cat and Elmer make plans for Wild Island.

_____ Elmer meets the gorilla.

_____ The boars discover someone is on their island.

_____ Elmer gives the tigers some chewing gum.

_____ Elmer rescues the baby dragon and they fly off together.

_____ Elmer leaves on the boat to the Isle of Tangerina.

_____ The crocodiles form a bridge for Elmer.

_____ Elmer wishes he could fly.

_____ Elmer meets the lion and gives him the ribbons for his mane.

_____ The mouse thinks Elmer's knapsack is a rock.

_____ Elmer brings the cat home and gets scolded by his mother.

_____ The rhinoceros tosses Elmer up and down on his tusk.

_____ The monkeys use the magnifying glasses to get the fleas off the gorilla.

_____ Elmer picks as many tangerines as he can.

Conversations

Cut the conversation strips and distribute one to each group of students. Have groups write and perform the conversation that might have occurred in each situation.

---

1. Elmer's mother scolds Elmer for bringing an "ugly, alley cat" home. (2 people)

---

2. Elmer says good-bye to the cat at the dock just before he leaves. (2 people)

---

3. The tigers talk about Elmer trespassing in their jungle and decide what to do about him. (7 people or less)

---

4. Elmer meets the lion and decides what to do about his messy mane. (2 people)

---

5. Before Elmer gives the magnifying glasses to the six little monkeys, they have to find the fleas on the gorilla whenever he asks. The monkeys are talking to one another about having to work whenever the gorilla asks them to. (4–5 people)

---

6. The monkeys are excited about the magnifying glasses and how much easier it is to find the fleas on the gorilla. (4–5 people)

---

7. Elmer is talking to himself, trying to figure out how to go about saving the baby dragon. (1 person)

---

8. Before Elmer spots the crocodiles, they see him and happily plot to get Elmer in the river. (1 person, plus any number of people—2 others or more)

---

9. The baby dragon is excitedly talking about being rescued when he sees Elmer coming to save him. (1 person)

---

10. Elmer and the baby dragon are flying over the island together, wondering where they will go. (2 people)

Objective Test and Essay

Matching: Match the problem with the animal by writing the letter on the line next to the animal.

1. _____ tigers   a. sweet tooth

2. _____ gorilla   b. tangled hair

3. _____ lion   c. fleas

4. _____ crocodiles   d. ugly tusk

5. _____ rhinoceros   e. hungry

True or False: Write *true* or *false* next to each statement below.

6. _____ On the way to the island, Elmer hid in a corn sack in the cargo hold of the ship.

7. _____ The wild boars were worried about an invasion.

8. _____ The dragon was placed on the island by a group of sailors.

9. _____ Elmer walked on the backs of turtles to get from the Isle of Tangerina to Wild Island.

10. _____ Elmer's mother was happy that her son brought a lonely cat home to take care of.

Short Answer: Write a short answer to the following questions.

11. Where did Elmer find the cat? _____

_____

12. Where did Elmer find the rhinoceros? _____

_____

13. What were the tigers going to do with Elmer? _____

_____

14. How did Elmer make his bridge? _____

_____

15. Where did Elmer and the baby dragon fly first when they left Wild Island? _____

_____

Essay: Write the answers to the following essay topics on the back of this paper.

1. Do you think that Elmer was respectful of his mother? Explain your answer.

2. Choose one of your favorite scenes from this story. Give three reasons why you chose this scene.

Bibliography and Related Reading

Books by Ruth Stiles Gannett

The Dragons of Blueland. Random House Childrens Pub., 1987.

Elmer and the Dragon. Random House Childrens Pub., 1987.

Other Books

Hadithi, Mwenye. *Baby Baboon.* Little, Brown & Co., 1993.

Hoff, Sydney. *Danny and the Dinosaur.* HarperCollins, 1999.

Lynne Cherry, Deborah. *The Great Kapok Tree.* Harcourt, 2000.

Mahy, Margaret. *17 Kings and 42 Elephants.* Dial Books for Young Readers, 1987.

Mahy, Margaret. *Simply Delicious!* Orchard Books, 1999.

Nolen, Jerdine. *Raising Dragons.* Harcourt, 1998.

Osborne, Mary Pope. *Tigers at Twilight.* Random House, 1999.

Rydell, Wendy. *All about Islands.* Troll Associates, 1984.

Tafuri, Nancy. *Junglewalk.* Greenwillow Books, 1988.

Wilson, Sarah. *Beware, the Dragons!* HarperCollins, 1988.

Wood, Audrey. *The Flying Dragon Room.* Scholastic, 2000.

Yaccarino, Dan. *Deep in the Jungle.* Atheneum Books for Young Readers, 2000.

Nonfiction

Amos, William Hopkins. *Wildlife of the Islands.* Abrams, 1980.

Gibbons, Gail. *Nature's Green Umbrella, Tropical Rain Forests.* Mulberry Books, 1997.

Greenaway, T. *Jungles: Eyewitness Books.* Alfred Knopf, 1994.

Grolier Educ. Group. *Amazing Animals of the World.* Grolier Inc., 1995.

Laycock, George. *Islands and Their Mysteries.* Four Winds Press, 1977.

O'Mara, A. *Rain Forests.* Capstone Press, 1996.

Ricciuti, E. *Jungles.* Western Publishing Co., 1984.

Technology

Let's Explore the Jungle. 1995.

The Dynamic Rainforest. Csiro Publishing, 1997.

The Jungle Book. Walt Disney, 1984.

Answer Key

Page 11

1. Accept appropriate responses.
2. Elmer met the cat on his street.
3. She didn't want the cat and thought that they would end up feeding all the stray cats.
4. Elmer told the cat that he wanted to fly more than anything else.
5. Isle of Tangerina and Wild Island
6. The cat told Elmer that the animals were very lazy and that they hated going all the way around to get to the other side.
7. The animals were going to use the flying baby dragon.
8. The baby dragon fell from the clouds to the bank of the river.
9. Responses will vary: chewing gum, two-dozen lollipops, a package of rubber bands, black rubber boots, a compass, a toothbrush and a tube of toothpaste, six magnifying glasses, a very sharp jackknife, a comb and a hairbrush, seven hair ribbons of different colors, an empty grain bag, clean clothes, twenty-five peanut butter and jelly sandwiches, and six apples.
10. Accept appropriate responses.

Page 16

1. Accept appropriate responses.
2. Elmer hid in the cargo hold in an empty grain (wheat) bag.
3. The merchant thought he felt corn cobs.
4. Elmer discovered a tangerine tree above his head.
5. He stepped onto the back of a sleeping whale.
6. He met a mouse.
7. The mouse thought Elmer's knapsack was a rock.
8. The second scary thing was walking between two wild boars.
9. The three signs of invasion were fresh tangerine peels under the wahoo bush, the "rock," and more peels.
10. Elmer learned to save his tangerine peels.

Page 22

1. Accept appropriate responses.
2. He got stuck in the mud.
3. He took out his compass.
4. He saw 14 eyes or 7 tigers.
5. Elmer was trespassing in their jungle, and they were hungry.
6. He gave them chewing gum that would grow into more gum if they chewed it long enough.
7. The boars greeted Elmer.
8. A rhinoceros was tossing him up and down because Elmer was trespassing.
9. He didn't like his ugly, yellow tusk.
10. Elmer gave him toothpaste and a toothbrush.

Page 24

1. fact	7. fiction	13. fiction
2. fact	8. fact	14. fact
3. fiction	9. fiction	15. fiction
4. fiction	10. fiction	16. fact
5. fact	11. fact	17. fact
6. fiction	12. fiction	18. fact

Page 27

1. Accept appropriate responses.
2. He met a lion yelling at himself.
3. The lion was yelling because of his tangled mane.
4. Elmer got out the comb, brush, and seven hair ribbons and then braided the lion's mane with ribbons.
5. He saw the lion's mother walking.
6. It was a big, black gorilla.
7. The gorilla was upset because he was scratching his fleas.
8. He called for the seven monkeys.
9. Elmer took out magnifying glasses and gave them to the monkeys to look for fleas.
10. The gorilla had all the monkeys on him searching for fleas.

Answer Key (cont.)

Page 32

1. Accept appropriate responses.
2. The gorilla would hear him and twist off his arm.
3. It was a crocodile and he wanted something sweet.
4. Elmer gave him a lollipop.
5. Elmer put a lollipop on the crocodile's tail. The other crocodiles lined up, making a bridge.
6. The wild boars were stepping onto the crocodile bridge and coming toward him.
7. He used his jackknife to cut the rope and free the baby dragon.
8. All the animals were standing on the backs of the crocodiles, and the crocodiles were smiling, ready to eat them.
9. Elmer and the baby dragon flew off to the Isle of Tangerina.
10. Responses will vary according to their understanding of the story.

Page 35

1. 36 animals
2. 10,125 pounds
3. 1,000 pounds
4. 2,516 pounds
5. 355 pounds
6. 40 years
7. 24 legs
8. 204 feet
9. 7 lollipops
10. 7 braids

Page 43

(6) Elmer walks across the rocks from the Isle of Tangerina to Wild Island.

(3) The alley cat and Elmer make plans for Wild Island.

(12) Elmer meets the gorilla.

(8) The boars discover someone is on their island.

(9) Elmer gives the tigers some chewing gum.

(15) Elmer rescues the baby dragon and they fly off together.

(4) Elmer leaves on the boat for the Isle of Tangerina.

(14) The crocodiles form a bridge for Elmer.

(2) Elmer wishes he could fly.

(11) Elmer meets the lion and gives him the ribbons for his mane.

(7) The mouse thinks Elmer's knapsack is a rock.

(1) Elmer brings the cat home and gets scolded by his mother.

(10) The rhinoceros tosses Elmer up and down on his tusk.

(13) The monkeys use the magnifying glasses to get the fleas off the gorilla.

(5) Elmer picks as many tangerines as he can.

Page 45

Matching

1. e
2. c
3. b
4. a
5. d

True or False

6. False. He hid in a wheat (grain) sack.
7. True. The wild boars were worried about an invasion on their island because of strange things.
8. False. The baby dragon fell out of a cloud.
9. False. Elmer walked on rocks to Wild Island.
10. False. Elmer's mother was very upset with him for bringing an ugly alley cat home.

Short Answer

11. Elmer found the cat on his street.
12. Elmer found the rhinoceros in the weeping pool.
13. The tigers were going to eat him because they were very hungry.
14. Elmer made his bridge on the backs of the crocodiles.
15. Elmer and the baby dragon flew to the Isle of Tangerina.

Essay

Answers will vary.